Notes for Architects

on the use and completion of the Domestic Project Pack

Royal Institute of British Architects

Notes for Architects

Use

The Domestic Project Pack contains Client and Architect copies of the Schedule of Architect's Services for a Domestic Project and the Conditions of Appointment for a Domestic Project, a draft Model Letter and notes about the Consumer Contracts Adjudication Scheme.

It also includes a copy of *Using an architect for your home*. This might help the less experienced client to understand the tasks ahead, the benefits of using an architect and what an architect can be expected to do and charge. A copy could be sent to the client in advance of face-to-face discussions on services and fees.

The Domestic Project Pack is particularly suitable for extensions and alterations where the building works will be carried out using appropriate forms of contract. Such contracts include:

- JCT Building Contract for a homeowner/occupier (HOC 05) – for works costing up to about £35,000 *, or
- JCT Agreement for Minor Works (MW 05) – for works costing up to about £150,000, or
- JCT Intermediate Form of Building Contract (IC 05), or
- ICE Conditions of Contract for Minor Works, 3rd edition, or
- CIOB Small Works Contract (2004 edition)
  * For a new house, a significant extension to an existing house or works to an historic house MW 05 or IC 05 may be most appropriate.

The Domestic Project Pack is used in conjunction with a specially drafted Letter of Appointment, signed under hand as a simple contract where the applicable law is the law of England or Northern Ireland. It is not suitable for use where the law of Scotland is applicable. Where the law of Northern Ireland is applicable in clause 12 delete 'England' and insert 'Northern Ireland'.

'Architect' is a protected title under the Architects Act 1997. The *RIBA Schedule of Architect's Services and Conditions for a Domestic Project* is therefore for use in the appointment of members of the Royal Institute of British Architects or other registered architects.

Client as 'consumer'

For work to his/her home the client will be a 'consumer', a term applied to a person 'acting for purposes which are outside his business', and the Unfair Terms in Consumer Contracts Regulations 1999 will apply. It is essential therefore to explain the Conditions and the Letter of Appointment and make whatever amendments are appropriate so that it can be agreed that all the terms have been individually negotiated in good faith.

The Model Letter of Appointment provides for disputes to be resolved with the agreement of the client, by negotiation, mediation, legal proceedings and/or non-statutory adjudication. It may be helpful to attach a copy of the notes on the adjudication scheme. 'Consumer Contracts' a paper on negotiating and other related matters is available to download at *www.architecture.com/membersonly*.

Note an architect when advising the Client about the building contract has an implied duty to draw attention to any provisions, e.g. statutory adjudication or payment notices, which may conflict with the *Unfair Terms* regulations.

Notes for Architects

The Schedule of Architect's Services

Tick the boxes in the printed Schedule for the Services required or enter 'T' for time charged services. The Schedule relates to a straightforward domestic project to be procured in the traditional manner. Although the Services are described in simple terms, performance must be '*in accordance with the normal standards of the Architect's profession*' (Clause 1.1).

If different or extra services are needed for the particular project, these can be described and identified as 'Other Services' in the space provided. Section 12.12 of the *Architect's Handbook of Practice Management* gives some useful advice about the risks associated with house inspection for the owner or a building society, etc.

The Conditions of Appointment

Cross through and initial any Conditions to be deleted or amended. If additional Conditions are absolutely essential, carefully consider their impact on the other Conditions; they may be set out on a separate sheet, initialled and appended to or included in the Letter of Appointment.

Note that the *Late Payment of Commercial Debts (Interest) Regulations 2002*, the *Housing Grants, Construction and Regeneration Act 1996* and the *CDM Regulations 1994* including the appointment of a Planning Supervisor do not apply to domestic clients. The interest rate in clause 5.2 is the same as that used in JCT contracts.

Letter of Appointment – completion and issue

The style or format of the letter is less important than its contents, which are necessary to complete the terms of the Appointment. Omission of any of the model contents should be carefully considered. The Model Letter of Appointment has been drafted to provide for project specific matters in conjunction with the Schedule and Conditions. For purposes of identification, insert accurate details of names and addresses and the nature and location of the Project. The Letter should be formal ('Dear Sir … Yours faithfully'.... 'for and on behalf of the Architect').

Refer to the numbered notes and adapt the model text as appropriate. [Items in square brackets are options or alternatives.] Delete those not required.

1 Make sure that all-important details relating to fees and expenses are included in the Letter. Fee options include percentage fees, a lump sum or sums or time based. *Note that the bases for percentage fees are set out in clause 4.3.*

   As appropriate, draw the client's attention to any items in the Services that will be time-charged and check that there is no inconsistency between the wording of the Letter and the specified Services.

   Stating the number of visits to construction works included in the quoted fee may provide a basis for negotiations if a greater number of visits prove to be advisable.

2 Where appropriate state the rates to apply to different people.

3 Where the net cost option applies state the rates for copies made in the office and the mileage rate for travel by car.

4 Professional indemnity insurance is a requirement for practice as an architect, but is not referred to in the Conditions and therefore should be covered in the Letter of Appointment.

Note the amount of PI insurance cover stated in the Letter is the amount to be available for the Project – the cap on liability – and should be based on assessment of the risk. The amount of cover may be less than that carried by the architect's practice. This in any case should be at least the amount required by the Architects Registration Board and include cover for legal defence costs.

5 The Consumer Contracts Adjudication scheme is operated under licence from JCT. The notes for guidance of the Client should be attached to the Letter of Appointment. A copy of the Rules is available from the Disputes Resolution Office, 66 Portland Place, London W1B 1AD.
Phone: 020 7307 3649   Fax: 020 7307 3754   email: adjudication@inst.riba.org

The Appointment is completed as a simple contract. It is not necessary to witness signatures to a simple contract unless either party requires confirmation of identity.

Either: Make up two sets of documents comprising the Letter and both copies of the Conditions and the Schedule of Architect's Services and the Adjudication notes. Sign the Agreement clause at the end of both copies of the Letter and initial both copies of the other documents and send to the client, who is asked to sign and initial each document including any amendment, and return the Architect's copies to you.

Or: Send the Letter of Appointment, the client's copy of the Conditions and the Schedule of Architect's Services and the Adjudication notes to the client for consideration and arrange a meeting when client and architect can meet to sign and initial the documents. *Don't forget to take the Architect's copies to the meeting!*

Published for the RIBA by RIBA Publishing, 15 Bonhill Street, London EC2P 2EA

First published February 2006

02.06 E D C B

Printed in Great Britain

Model Letter

for a Domestic Project

Available to download as a text document at
www.architecture.com/membersonly

Royal Institute of British Architects

Model Letter for a Domestic Project

From architect to client on practice notepaper and addressed to the client's permanent address.

Dear [Mr] [and Mrs] ______________

Proposed [Project] [building work] at ______________

Thank you for inviting me/us to act as your architect for [your new home] [the alterations and extension to your home] [as described] [in your letter of _____] [on the attached sheet].

You told me/us that your target cost for the building work is £ __________ to which must be added our fees and any VAT. You also said that you would like building works to [commence on] [be complete by] ______________________

I/We [have agreed] [proposed] that the basis for our appointment should be:

- the *Conditions of Appointment for a Domestic Project;* and
- the *Schedule of Architect's Services for a Domestic Project*

I/we explained the meaning of the Conditions and this letter and discussed the Services which appeared appropriate for your project. My/Our Services are to be performed in the 'Before Construction' stages [and in the subsequent Construction stages.] [You told me/us that you will obtain tenders and oversee the building work.] If it becomes necessary to vary the Services we will let you know and we can discuss how this might be arranged.

[As your project involves a common wall with your neighbour I will draft the initial Party Structure notice, for you to submit to the neighbour with a reply form but any other services will be charged on a time basis.]

The Schedule and Conditions completed as we discussed which with this letter will, if you agree, record the terms of our agreement.

[At this time I/we do not believe it will be necessary to seek advice from any other consultants, but if this should change I/we will advise you about the requirements and the fees entailed.]

[I/we have informed you that I/we shall require the services of [a structural engineer] [quantity surveyor]. I/we will write separately about their appointment and the fees entailed.]

[As agreed with you I/we will engage ____________ a firm of [structural engineers] [quantity surveyors] to advise me/us. I/we shall be responsible to you for their services, the costs of which are included in my/our fee.]

Fee

[1] My/Our fee [in the Before Construction period for the Preparation, Design [and Construction Information] stage(s)] will be ______________________________ [and for the Construction stages will be ______________________________ , which includes for [number of] visits to the site in connection with our duties during construction.]

[2] [Time based services, identified by "T" in the Schedule and] any extra services will be charged at £_____ per hour. [For such Services I/we will obtain your consent before providing more than ___ hours in the Before Construction stages] [and ___ hours in the Construction stages.]

Before implementing any changes to the Services or design I/we will agree with you any consequential change to our fee.

[3] [In addition to the fee the following expenses will be charged] [at net cost] [plus a handling charge of __%] [by the addition of __% to the total fee] [list expenses.]

[My/Our fee includes my/our expenses.] [but excludes any disbursements ...] Any disbursements made on your behalf, such as payments to the local authority for planning submissions or Building Regulations approval [which] will be charged at net cost [plus a handling charge of__%.]

[I am/we are registered for VAT, which is chargeable on all fees and expenses.] [VAT is not chargeable on my/our accounts as I am/we are not registered, but if during the course of this appointment it is necessary to register for VAT this will change.]

I/We will submit an account for the fees and any expenses or disbursements due [plus VAT] [each month] [on completion of each work stage] in accordance with Condition 5.2. [Monthly accounts will be based on the estimated percentage of completion.] Payment should be made within 30 days.

Liability and insurance

[4] The maximum limit of my/our liability to you in contract, tort or statutory duty for any one claim or series of claims arising from one event on this project is limited to £ _________, this is the amount [of your target cost for the building work] [required by the Architects Registration Board]. Any such liability will expire after six years from completion of the Services.

I/We shall maintain professional indemnity insurance cover for this amount until the expiry of our liability. I/We should be pleased to provide documentary evidence of the insurance, if required.

Disputes

In the event of a dispute or difference arising under this Appointment I/we hope we shall be able to settle the matter by negotiation or mediation. Alternatively, either of us can start court proceedings to settle the dispute at any time.

[5] Or either of us can have disputes decided within 21 days by an adjudicator appointed under the Consumer Adjudication scheme, for which notes are attached.

[6] **Either:** I/We enclose an additional copy of this letter and 2 copies of the Conditions for a Domestic Project and the Schedule of Services. We have signed and initialled all the documents where required and would ask you to sign and initial them where indicated and return our copies to me/us.

Or: I/We enclose a copy of the Conditions and the Schedule of Architect's Services. When you have read them through I/we will arrange a meeting when we could sign and initial them to complete our agreement. I/We will bring our copies to the meeting.

Yours faithfully

For and on behalf of the [Architect]

Agreement

The Client wishes to appoint the Architect to perform Services for the building work and the Architect has agreed to accept the appointment and to perform the Services subject to the terms set out in this Letter of Appointment and the attached copy of the RIBA *Schedule of Architect's Services for a Domestic Project* and *Conditions of Appointment for a Domestic Project* as completed.

[5] *Signed* *(Client)* ______________________ (date) ____________

Signed *(Architect)* ______________________ (date) ____________

Principal RIBA Membership no: ______________________

ARB Registration no: ______________________

Published for the RIBA by RIBA Publishing, 15 Bonhill Street, London EC2P 2EA

First published February 2006

02.06 E D C B

Printed in Great Britain

Client's copy

Schedule of Architect's Services

for a Domestic Project

Royal Institute of British Architects

Schedule of Architect's Services for a Domestic Project

Tick the boxes for the Services required or enter 'T' for time-based services

BEFORE CONSTRUCTION

Preparation

- Visit the property and carry out an initial appraisal
- Assist the Client in preparing the Client's requirements
- Identify alternative solutions for the project
- Advise on the need for services by consultants or specialists

Design

- Survey and prepare drawings of site and/or buildings as required
- Arrange investigation of soil or structural conditions
- Prepare a preliminary design and discuss with the Client
- Develop the final design
- Prepare an approximate estimate of cost
- Submit the final design proposals and approximate cost for approval
- Make an application for detailed planning permission

Construction Information

Delete the option not applicable

- Co-ordinate and integrate any designs provided by others
- Prepare drawings and other information required for construction
- Prepare: (a) a specification (b) schedule of works
- Make an application for Building Regulations approval
- Advise on an appropriate form of building contract, its conditions and the responsibilities of the Client, the Architect and the builder

Schedule of Architect's Services for a Domestic Project

Other Services

These activities do not form part of the Services unless identified as 'Other Services' above:

- Models and special drawings
- Exceptional negotiations in connection with statutory requirements
- Submission of proposals for approval of landlords, freeholders, etc.
- Preparing a schedule of dilapidations
- Services in connection with party wall negotiations
- Services in any dispute between the Client and another party
- Services in connection with government and other grants

CONSTRUCTION

Tender action

Prepare documents required for tendering purposes

Advise on builders to be invited to tender for the work

Invite, appraise and report on tenders

Construction work

Advise on the appointment of a builder

Prepare the building contract and arrange for it to be signed

Provide the builder with the information required for construction

Visit the site to see that the work is proceeding generally in accordance with the contract

Certify payments for work carried out or completed.
Advise on anticipated final cost

Provide or obtain record drawings showing the building and its services, and give general advice on maintenance

After hand-over

- Make final inspections and arrange for correction of any defects
- Settle final account and issue a final certificate

Other Services

These activities do not form part of the Services unless identified as 'Other Services' above:

- Exceptional negotiations in connection with statutory requirements
- Submission of proposals for approval of landlords, freeholders, etc.
- Negotiating a price with a builder (in lieu of tendering)
- Services in connection with party wall negotiations
- Services in any dispute between the Client and another party
- Services following damage by fire and other causes

Signed	Client	
	Architect	

Published for the RIBA by RIBA Publishing, 15 Bonhill Street, London EC2P 2EA

First published February 2006

02.06 E D C B

Printed in Great Britain

Architect's copy

Schedule of Architect's Services

for a Domestic Project

Royal Institute of British Architects

Schedule of Architect's Services for a Domestic Project

Tick the boxes for the Services required or enter 'T' for time-based services

BEFORE CONSTRUCTION

Preparation

- [ ] Visit the property and carry out an initial appraisal
- [ ] Assist the Client in preparing the Client's requirements
- [ ] Identify alternative solutions for the project
- [ ] Advise on the need for services by consultants or specialists
- [ ]
- [ ]
- [ ]

Design

- [ ] Survey and prepare drawings of site and/or buildings as required
- [ ] Arrange investigation of soil or structural conditions
- [ ] Prepare a preliminary design and discuss with the Client
- [ ] Develop the final design
- [ ] Prepare an approximate estimate of cost
- [ ] Submit the final design proposals and approximate cost for approval
- [ ] Make an application for detailed planning permission
- [ ]
- [ ]
- [ ]

Construction Information

Delete the option not applicable

- [ ] Co-ordinate and integrate any designs provided by others
- [ ] Prepare drawings and other information required for construction
- [ ] Prepare: (a) a specification (b) schedule of works
- [ ] Make an application for Building Regulations approval
- [ ] Advise on an appropriate form of building contract, its conditions and the responsibilities of the Client, the Architect and the builder
- [ ]
- [ ]
- [ ]

Schedule of Architect's Services for a Domestic Project

Other Services

These activities do not form part of the Services unless identified as 'Other Services' above:

- Models and special drawings
- Exceptional negotiations in connection with statutory requirements
- Submission of proposals for approval of landlords, freeholders, etc.
- Preparing a schedule of dilapidations
- Services in connection with party wall negotiations
- Services in any dispute between the Client and another party
- Services in connection with government and other grants

CONSTRUCTION

Tender action

Prepare documents required for tendering purposes

Advise on builders to be invited to tender for the work

Invite, appraise and report on tenders

Construction work

Advise on the appointment of a builder

Prepare the building contract and arrange for it to be signed

Provide the builder with the information required for construction

Visit the site to see that the work is proceeding generally in accordance with the contract

Certify payments for work carried out or completed.
Advise on anticipated final cost

Provide or obtain record drawings showing the building and its services, and give general advice on maintenance

After hand-over

- Make final inspections and arrange for correction of any defects
- Settle final account and issue a final certificate

Other Services

These activities do not form part of the Services unless identified as 'Other Services' above:

- Exceptional negotiations in connection with statutory requirements
- Submission of proposals for approval of landlords, freeholders, etc.
- Negotiating a price with a builder (in lieu of tendering)
- Services in connection with party wall negotiations
- Services in any dispute between the Client and another party
- Services following damage by fire and other causes

Signed	Client	
	Architect	

Published for the RIBA by RIBA Publishing, 15 Bonhill Street, London EC2P 2EA

First published February 2006

02.06 E D C B

Printed in Great Britain

Client's copy

Conditions of Appointment

for a Domestic Project

Royal Institute of British Architects

Conditions of Appointment for a Domestic Project

Architect's Services

1 The Architect shall:

.1 exercise reasonable skill and care in performing the Services in accordance with the normal standards of the Architect's profession;

.2 act as the Client's representative and act fairly when dealing between Client and any other party;

.3 advise on compliance with statutory requirements;

.4 co-operate with any other persons appointed, co-ordinate and integrate their work and pass relevant information to them;

.5 make no material alteration to the Services or the approved design without the consent of the Client, except in an emergency;

.6 advise on progress in the performance of the Services and of any issue that may affect the programme for or the cost or quality of the project;

.7 not sub-contract performance of any part of the Services without the consent of the Client, which consent shall not be unreasonably withheld.

2 The Architect cannot guarantee that any target or budget cost or the timetable will be met, particularly where approvals from other parties, such as planning permission, are required, nor the performance, work or the products of others.

Client's responsibilities

3 The Client shall:

.1 advise the Architect of the requirements and of any subsequent changes required;

.2 provide accurate information necessary for the proper and timely performance of the Services, and the Architect shall rely on such information;

.3 give decisions and approvals necessary for the performance of the Services;

.4 have authority to issue instructions to the Architect, subject to the Architect's right of reasonable objection;

.5 appoint and pay any consultants or contractors required under separate agreements;

.6 not deal with the contractor or contractors directly or interfere with the Architect's duties or actions under the building contract;

.7 hold the contractor or contractors responsible for the proper carrying out and completion of construction works and for health and safety provisions on the site.

Copyright and licence

4 The Architect owns the copyright in the drawings and documents produced in performing the Services. The Client shall have a licence to copy and use them only for purposes related to the Project providing that all fees and/or other amounts due are paid in accordance with clause 5.2.

Fees

5 .1 The Architect's fees shall be calculated and charged as set out in the Letter of Appointment;

.2 The Client shall pay the Architect's accounts, including any additional fees, expenses, disbursements or VAT, within 30 days from the date of issue. Any sums remaining unpaid after 30 days shall bear interest at 5% over Bank of England Base Rate;

.3 Where a percentage basis applies, the percentage or percentages stated in the Letter of Appointment shall be applied to the final cost of the building work, excluding VAT, fees and any claims made by or against the contractor or contractors. The percentages will be applied to the current cost estimate, or the lowest acceptable tender, or the contract sum until the final cost has been ascertained;

.4 Additional fees shall be payable if the Architect for reasons beyond the Architect's control, is involved in extra work or incurs extra expense;

.5 The Architect shall be entitled to payment of any part of the fee for services satisfactorily performed together with any other amounts due at the date of any notice suspending or ending performance of any or all of the Services.

Expenses

6 The Client shall reimburse expenses and disbursements as stated in the Letter of Appointment.

Records

7 The Architect shall keep and make available on request records of any expenses and disbursements to be reimbursed at net cost and/or of time spent on Services charged on a time basis.

Assignment of the Agreement

8 .1 Neither the Client or the Architect shall assign the benefits or obligations or all of the Agreement without the consent of the other;

.2 Unless any part or all of the Agreement is transferred with consent to another person, nothing in this Agreement shall confer or purport to confer on any third party, any benefit or right to enforce any term of this Agreement.

Suspending or ending the Agreement

9 The Client or the Architect can suspend or end performance of any or all of the Services by giving at least 7 days' written notice of the intention and stating the reason for doing so.

If the reason for the notice arises from a default and the recipient does not remedy the matter, the agreement will end on expiry of the notice period.

Where Services are suspended by the Client and not resumed within 3 months the Architect shall have the right to treat performance of the Services affected as ended on giving written notice to the Client.

Architect's continuing liability

10 The Architect shall be liable for any consequences of failing to keep to this Agreement for six years from completion of the Services.

Dispute resolution

11 Resolution of any dispute or difference arising out of the Appointment shall be dealt with as set out in the Letter of Appointment.

Architects are subject to the disciplinary sanction of the Architects Registration Board in relation to unacceptable professional conduct or serious professional incompetence.

Governing law

12 The law applicable to this Agreement shall be the law of England.

Signed	Client	
	Architect	

Published for the RIBA by RIBA Publishing, 15 Bonhill Street, London EC2P 2EA

First published February 2006

02.06 E D C B

Printed in Great Britain

Architect's copy

Conditions of Appointment

for a Domestic Project

Royal Institute of British Architects

Conditions of Appointment for a Domestic Project

Architect's Services

1 The Architect shall:

.1 exercise reasonable skill and care in performing the Services in accordance with the normal standards of the Architect's profession;

.2 act as the Client's representative and act fairly when dealing between Client and any other party;

.3 advise on compliance with statutory requirements;

.4 co-operate with any other persons appointed, co-ordinate and integrate their work and pass relevant information to them;

.5 make no material alteration to the Services or the approved design without the consent of the Client, except in an emergency;

.6 advise on progress in the performance of the Services and of any issue that may affect the programme or the cost or quality of the project;

.7 not sub-contract performance of any part of the Services without the consent of the Client, which consent shall not be unreasonably withheld.

2 The Architect cannot guarantee that any target or budget cost or the timetable will be met, particularly where approvals from other parties, such as planning permission, are required, nor the performance, work or the products of others.

Client's responsibilities

3 The Client shall:

.1 advise the Architect of the requirements and of any subsequent changes required;

.2 provide accurate information necessary for the proper and timely performance of the Services, and the Architect shall rely on such information;

.3 give decisions and approvals necessary for the performance of the Services;

.4 have authority to issue instructions to the Architect, subject to the Architect's right of reasonable objection;

.5 appoint and pay any consultants or contractors required under separate agreements;

.6 not deal with the contractor or contractors directly or interfere with the Architect's duties or actions under the building contract;

.7 hold the contractor or contractors responsible for the proper carrying out and completion of construction works and for health and safety provisions on the site.

Copyright and licence

4 The Architect owns the copyright in the drawings and documents produced in performing the Services. The Client shall have a licence to copy and use them only for purposes related to the Project providing that all fees and/or other amounts due are paid in accordance with clause 5.2.

Fees

5 .1 The Architect's fees shall be calculated and charged as set out in the Letter of Appointment;

.2 The Client shall pay the Architect's accounts, including any additional fees, expenses, disbursements or VAT, within 30 days from the date of issue. Any sums remaining unpaid after 30 days shall bear interest at 5% over Bank of England Base Rate;

.3 Where a percentage basis applies, the percentage or percentages stated in the Letter of Appointment shall be applied to the final cost of the building work, excluding VAT, fees and any claims made by or against the contractor or contractors. The percentages will be applied to the current cost estimate, or the lowest acceptable tender, or the contract sum until the final cost has been ascertained;

.4 Additional fees shall be payable if the Architect for reasons beyond the Architect's control, is involved in extra work or incurs extra expense;

.5 The Architect shall be entitled to payment of any part of the fee for services satisfactorily performed together with any other amounts due at the date of any notice suspending or ending performance of any or all of the Services.

Expenses

6 The Client shall reimburse expenses and disbursements as stated in the Letter of Appointment.

Records

7 The Architect shall keep and make available on request records of any expenses and disbursements to be reimbursed at net cost and/or of time spent on Services charged on a time basis.

Assignment of the Agreement

8 .1 Neither the Client or the Architect shall assign the benefits or obligations or all of the Agreement without the consent of the other;

.2 Unless any part or all of the Agreement is transferred with consent to another person, nothing in this Agreement shall confer or purport to confer on any third party, any benefit or right to enforce any term of this Agreement.

Suspending or ending the Agreement

9 The Client or the Architect can suspend or end performance of any or all of the Services by giving at least 7 days' written notice of the intention and stating the reason for doing so.

If the reason for the notice arises from a default and the recipient does not remedy the matter, the agreement will end on expiry of the notice period.

Where Services are suspended by the Client and not resumed within 3 months the Architect shall have the right to treat performance of the Services affected as ended on giving written notice to the Client.

Architect's continuing liability

10 The Architect shall be liable for any consequences of failing to keep to this Agreement for six years from completion of the Services.

Dispute resolution

11 Resolution of any dispute or difference arising out of the Appointment shall be dealt with as set out in the Letter of Appointment.

Architects are subject to the disciplinary sanction of the Architects Registration Board in relation to unacceptable professional conduct or serious professional incompetence.

Governing law

12 The law applicable to this Agreement shall be the law of England.

Signed	Client	
	Architect	

Published for the RIBA by RIBA Publishing, 15 Bonhill Street, London EC2P 2EA

First published February 2006

02.06 E D C B

Printed in Great Britain

Using an architect for your home

Royal Institute of British Architects

Using an architect for your home

Whether you are planning to build a new house, to alter or extend your present home, to employ a builder or just do it yourself, it makes sense to consult an architect.

This guide is designed to show how an architect can help, the benefits to your project, and how working with an architect can pave the way to a successful project.

Why you need an architect

An RIBA Chartered Architect will provide you with much more than just the drawings for your new home or alteration. You will be fully involved in creating a totally tailored solution for your living needs. An architect has the experience to steer your project safely through to completion, overseeing the design, planning and building regulations, the builders and your budget.

You can hire an architect to manage any or all parts of the design and construction process. All architects are trained to:

- help you to **define your objectives** for the project, identify the risks involved and interpret your ideas imaginatively and expertly;
- work with you to **develop a design** that will maximise your investment, be economic to build and run, and, of course, bring you years of comfort and pleasure;
- help to **secure the approvals** that will be needed before your project can go ahead, including the preparation of applications to the local authority for planning consent (which certifies that the project meets rules governing the use and form of buildings) and for Building Regulations certification (which covers the functional requirements of buildings to safeguard the health and safety of the people using them);
- be able to **manage the construction phase** by helping you to select suitable builders, obtain competitive prices for construction, monitor progress, standards and safety on-site, arrange the input of other design specialists, and oversee the co-ordination of the construction through to its successful completion.

Setting your brief

Your brief should be clear and unambiguous and it should enshrine a common understanding between you and your architect.

Seek the architect's help in formulating the brief. The process may involve a number of discussions and help to establish the dialogue between you that the project needs. Above all the project brief should describe:

- The functions of the finished project
  Who will use it, and for what?
  Have you visualised how these activities will be accommodated and provided for in the new space(s)?

- Your motivations and expectations
  What do you hope to achieve by this project, in the short and long term, for yourself and others?

- A design direction
  Contrasting or in keeping with existing buildings?
  Contemporary or traditional?
  Are there certain materials, fixtures or finishes you favour?
  Is sustainability an issue for you?

- Authority for decision making
  Who will sign off decisions about design, about costs and about day-to-day matters on-site?

- Timetables and budgets
  When should key stages be completed, how much should they cost, and how will they be financed?

A good, thorough brief will form the basis of the professional agreement you sign with your architect.

Protecting your interests

You are likely to be making a large financial and emotional commitment to your project, which makes standards and performance from others all the more important. Using a Chartered Architect provides you with extra safeguards to ensure that your designer acts with integrity and gives independent advice in support of your interests.

Only qualified architects registered with the Architects Registration Board are entitled to call themselves 'architects' in the UK and only registered architects who are members of RIBA and adhere to the RIBA *Code of Professional Conduct* can be called 'Chartered Architects'.

If you are uncertain about the credentials of anyone claiming to be a Chartered Architect do ask them for their RIBA membership number or check with the RIBA.

Architects are required by UK law to be registered with the Architects Registration Board (ARB) and to comply with the Board's *Standards of Conduct and Practice*.

The ARB also has an obligation to represent consumers' interests and in the final resort architects are subject to the disciplinary sanction of the Board in respect of 'unacceptable professional conduct or serious professional incompetence'.

The requirements of the RIBA and ARB codes of Professional Conduct include:

- maintenance of professional indemnity insurance cover appropriate to the scale and type of work undertaken;
- provision of adequate competence and resources; and
- a written record of the agreement with the client.

The client/architect agreement

Once you have selected your architect, the responsibilities of each party and the services to be provided by the architect should be set down in a formal agreement.

When you have work done to your home, you are acting in your private capacity, i.e. as a 'consumer', which is where the *Unfair Terms of Consumer Contracts Regulations 1999* come into play. Your architect will discuss these issues with you so the terms of your agreement are fully understood and 'individually negotiated in good faith'.

The agreement will record:

- details of your project and the services to be provided by the architect;
- the calculation of fees and expenses;
- the appointment of any other consultants;
- the amount of the architect's insurance cover and period of liability; and
- dispute resolution procedures.

You may find the RIBA *Conditions of Appointment* and *Schedule of Architect's Services* will be suitable for this purpose. These state, in plain, simple terms, the basic responsibilities of the architect, which include:

- performing the services required using reasonable skill and care;
- acting as your representative;
- advising you on compliance with statutory requirements;

- keeping you updated on progress and on issues affecting time, cost or quality;
- not making any material changes, without your agreement, to the services or the agreed design except in an emergency; and
- not sub-contracting any obligation under the agreement.

When you have discussed and agreed all the details, your architect will draft a Letter of Agreement which you both sign to complete the contract.

Fees and expenses

There is no standard or recommended basis for this calculation and the fee is usually a matter for negotiation. The fee will reflect the degree of personal service and bespoke design that your project involves. Other factors will include the location and size of the practice, its reputation and specialist skills.

In 2004, an independent annual survey of fees by Mirza & Nacey Research recorded the general level of architect's fees for providing a full service for new private houses to be between 8% and 12% of the construction cost. On projects to refurbish or extend houses, or for repair and conservation work on historic buildings, the fee can be a larger percentage of the building cost.

Fees for a partial service for preparing the design and submitting the planning application are generally between 3% and 5% of the construction cost.

Fee options

An architect will usually quote their fee as a percentage of the building cost or as a lump sum. In cases where the scope of their work is harder to predict, or for services such as surveys or party wall services, the quote will usually consist of an hourly or daily rate together with an estimate of the time required.

Expenses

These will generally be added to the fee and will be charged for items such as the costs of travel, copying drawings and documents, and for making planning or Building Regulations applications.

Payment

An architect who is retained for the entire project will typically invoice about one third of the fee during the design stage, the same at the construction information stage, and the balance during and following construction. Invoices are usually issued monthly, but regular payments can be budgeted over a period. Alternatively, fees might be paid on completion of each work stage.

Legislation

It is important, before you start your project, that you are aware of the approvals that will be needed from the local authority for Planning and Building Regulations, as well as legislation that might affect your plans, such as party wall regulations.

Your architect can guide you through all of these matters as they develop the design. They will also be able to make the necessary submissions for approvals and handle negotiations with the statutory bodies.

The building contract

This is a vital document – the legally binding commitment between you, as the client, and your builder to deliver your project. Your architect can administer this contract on your behalf.

As we all know, it is not uncommon for building projects to contain hidden surprises – structural quirks or unexpected ground conditions, for example – that can impact on the design and possibly on the building cost. The best way to prepare yourself is an adequate written contract, designed to manage such events fairly from each party's point of view.

There is a range of standard forms of contract tailored to different size projects, and your architect will be able to advise you on the one best suited to your needs. They can also explain your rights under the *Unfair Terms in Consumer Contracts Regulations 1999*, and how these might influence your decisions about certain terms in the building contract, particularly payment procedures and dispute resolution.

Published for the RIBA by RIBA Publishing, 15 Bonhill Street, London EC2P 2EA

First published February 2006

02.06 E D C B

Printed in Great Britain

Consumer Contracts Adjudication Scheme

Royal Institute of British Architects

Consumer Contracts Adjudication Scheme

Choosing adjudication

Where a dispute between someone having work to his/her home, i.e. 'a consumer', and a contractor or a professional advisor cannot be resolved by the parties, the option of adjudication may provide a relatively quick solution, instead of the more expensive and lengthy alternatives of arbitration or litigation.

Adjudication is a procedure where a single issue dispute between the parties is decided by an impartial third party (the adjudicator).

There is no compulsion for a 'consumer' to adopt adjudication, although it is included in most contracts. Under the *Unfair Terms in Consumer Regulations 1999 'the consumer's right to take legal action or exercise any other legal remedy'* must not be excluded or hindered by the contract terms. The effect of this is that the consumer should choose or be aware of the available dispute resolution procedures.

The Royal Institute of British Architects (RIBA), the Royal Institution of Chartered Surveyors (RICS) and the National Specialist Contractors Council (NSCC) provide a Consumer Contracts Adjudication service suitable for the majority of domestic projects, where statutory adjudication does not apply.

Most standard contracts incorporate procedures for statutory adjudication which applies to all construction contracts, including professional appointments, except for domestic projects.

The choice of the 'consumer' or the 'statutory' procedures may depend on the degree of risk or complexity of the project, which will also be reflected in the choice of the appropriate form of building contract or the agreement for professional services.

The following notes apply to the Consumer Contracts Scheme.

The adjudicator

Either party can apply to any of the appointing bodies to appoint the adjudicator. He/She will be selected from an approved panel of adjudicators to reflect his/her knowledge and experience of the subject matter of the dispute, e.g. quality of work or materials, payments, etc. When an adjudicator has been appointed, both parties will be notified, in writing, by the appointing body. They will be told who the adjudicator is and that the adjudicator will contact both parties directly.

What will it cost?

If either party wants to have a dispute decided by an adjudicator he/she must complete an application form, available from RIBA, RICS or NSCC, and return it with a payment of £117.50 (inclusive of VAT) to the preferred appointing body. (The payment covers the administration costs.)

The adjudicator will charge an hourly fee for his/her services. He/She will tell the consumer and the supplier, before he/she begins the adjudication, what his/her fee will be. The amount of the fee will depend upon the complexity of the issues in dispute, but will not exceed £95 per hour (inclusive of VAT) for the first 10 hours. This is regardless of how many additional hours the adjudicator actually spends on the adjudication.

Consumer Contracts Adjudication Scheme

What will the adjudicator do?

The adjudicator will invite each party, who may be represented by a lawyer or other advisor, to give their views about the dispute and what decision they think the adjudicator should reach. This will usually take the form of brief written statements. The adjudicator may require to inspect the works and to put questions directly to the parties.The adjudicator will consider matters brought to his/her attention by the parties, in writing or verbally, and may also make independent investigations and use personal expertise to ascertain the matters he/she considers necessary for reaching a decision.

How long does it take?

The objective of the adjudication procedure is to resolve the dispute within 28 days from the day an application for the adjudicator is received by the appointing body. Once an application is received by the appointing body, an adjudicator will normally be appointed within 7 days (including weekends but excluding public holidays). Once the adjudicator is appointed he/she will reach a decision within 21 days (including weekends but excluding public holidays). In many cases the adjudicator may be able to make a decision sooner, particularly if the issue in dispute is straightforward.

The adjudicator's decision

The decision of the adjudicator is final and binding unless it is referred for a final decision to the court. The adjudicator will write to both parties informing them of the decision and asking for payment of his/her fee.

The adjudicator's decision will be final and binding and will remain so unless and until it is finally decided in court proceedings. Either party may refer the matter to court at any time.

A copy of the Rules and an application form to appoint an adjudicator are available from:

Royal Institute of British Architects
Disputes Resolution Office
66 Portland Place
London W1B 1AD
Tel: 020 7307 3649
Fax: 020 7307 3793
email: adjudication@inst.riba.org

Royal Institution of Chartered Surveyors
Dispute Resolution Service
Westwood Way
Coventry CV4 8JE
Tel: 020 7222 7000
Fax: 020 7334 3802
email: drs@rics.org.uk

National Specialists Contractors Council
Carthusian Court
12 Carthusian Street
London EC2A 4JX
Tel: 0870 429 6351
Fax: 0870 429 6352
email: enquiries@nscc.org.uk

Published for the RIBA by RIBA Publishing, 15 Bonhill Street, London EC2P 2EA

First published February 2006

02.06 E D C B

Printed in Great Britain